THIS JOURNAL BELONGS TO:

_____

IF LOST, PLEASE CONTACT ME AT:

_____

_____

_____

Notes

DATE STARTED: 7/26/20

PROJECT:_____

MATERIALS

BASE MATERIAL AND SIZE:_____

COLORS

DIOXATINE PURPLE + FLOE TROL —THIN
IRIDECENT WHITE + TITANIUM WHITE + UV BLUE + FLOE
NEON YELLOW + BRILLIANT Y/G + FLOE + SUAVE OIL
BRILLIANT BLUE + HALOGAD + LUBE + FLOE

ADDITIVES

TECHNIQUES USED

FLIP CUP

CURING TIME/COMPLETED _____

FINISH MATERIALS/TECHNIQUE
DRAGONFLY TOPCOAT

COMPLETED: _____

GOOD RESULTS!!

Notes

DATE STARTED: _____

PROJECT:_____

MATERIALS

BASE MATERIAL AND SIZE:_____

COLORS

MED MAGENTA + FLORECENT PINK + FLOE + OIL
PRE MIXED IRIDECENT WHITE ARTIST LOFT
BRILLIANT Y/O + NEON YELLOW + FLOE + OIL
DIOXATINE PURPLE +

BAD COMBO

ADDITIVES

HAIR OIL
FLOE TROL

TECHNIQUES USED

FLIP CUP

CURING TIME/COMPLETED _____

FINISH MATERIALS/TECHNIQUE

_____
_____
_____

COMPLETED: _____

Notes

ADDED DARK
TEAL AND
THAT WAS GOOD

DATE STARTED: _____

PROJECT:_____

MATERIALS

BASE MATERIAL AND SIZE:_____ LATEX
↑

COLORS

OPAQUE NEON YELLOW   NOT A LOT, COUPLE
BLACK, THIN INK + FLOE
TRANSPARENT WHITE + IRIDECENT MEDIUM
DIOXAZINE PURPLE + FLOE
TURQUOISE + LATEX + FLOE
PHTHALOCYANINE GREEN + HALO BLUE GOLD + LATEX

ADDITIVES

TECHNIQUES USED

Transparent White, NOT Opaque !!

FLIP CUP GOOD

ADD COUPLE DROPS OF LATEX BETWEEN
LAYERS

CURING TIME/COMPLETED _____

FINISH MATERIALS/TECHNIQUE

COMPLETED: _____

Notes

BLACK AND WHITE SHOULD GO
NEXT TO EACH OTHER IN THE
CUP

YELLOW NEXT TO WHITE IN CUP

TAKE UR DAMN TIME.

LET THE CUP SIT BEFOE
PULLING

DATE STARTED: 1/20/22

PROJECT: _____

MATERIALS

BASE MATERIAL AND SIZE: 4 x 4 DEEP CANVASS

COLORS

FOLK ART COLOR SHIFT AQUA FLASH
FOLK ART COLOR SHIFT GREEN FLASH

LIGHT BLUE + TURQUOISE DEEP INK
DIOXAZINE PURPLE   LIQUITEX
BRILLIANT PURPLE   ARTIST LOFT

ADD DIOXAZINE   NEON YELLOW INK
                              IN LIGHT
ADDITIVES   COLORS

SUAVE MORROCCAN HAIR OIL
ARTIST LOFT SILICONE OIL
       TO LIGHT COLORS ONLY
FLOE IN ALL COLORS
TECHNIQUES USED
FLIP CUP

_____
_____
_____
_____
_____

CURING TIME/COMPLETED _____

FINISH MATERIALS/TECHNIQUE

_____
_____
_____

COMPLETED: _____

Notes

DATE STARTED: _July 9 2022_

PROJECT:_____

MATERIALS

BASE MATERIAL AND SIZE:_____

COLORS

DRIZZLE AQUA   + SILICONE
DRIZZLE LAVENDER   + SILICONE + UV
DRIZZLE PHALO BLU   + SILICONE
DRIZZLE BLD OR
DRIZZL WHITE
_____
_____

ADDITIVES

ARTIST LOFT SILICONE
_____
_____

TECHNIQUES USED

FLIP CUP + DRAG
_____
_____
_____
_____

CURING TIME/COMPLETED _____

FINISH MATERIALS/TECHNIQUE
_____
_____
_____

COMPLETED: _____

Notes

DATE STARTED: _____

PROJECT:_____

MATERIALS

BASE MATERIAL AND SIZE:_____

COLORS

_____
_____
_____
_____
_____
_____
_____

ADDITIVES

_____
_____
_____

TECHNIQUES USED

_____
_____
_____
_____
_____

CURING TIME/COMPLETED _____

FINISH MATERIALS/TECHNIQUE

_____
_____
_____

COMPLETED: _____

Notes

DATE STARTED: _____

PROJECT:_____

MATERIALS

BASE MATERIAL AND SIZE:_____

COLORS

_____
_____
_____
_____
_____
_____
_____
_____

ADDITIVES

_____
_____
_____

TECHNIQUES USED

_____
_____
_____
_____
_____

CURING TIME/COMPLETED _____

FINISH MATERIALS/TECHNIQUE

_____
_____
_____

COMPLETED: _____

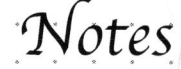
Notes

DATE STARTED: _____

PROJECT:_____

MATERIALS

BASE MATERIAL AND SIZE:_____

COLORS

_____
_____
_____
_____
_____
_____
_____

ADDITIVES

_____
_____
_____

TECHNIQUES USED

_____
_____
_____
_____
_____

CURING TIME/COMPLETED _____

FINISH MATERIALS/TECHNIQUE

_____
_____
_____

COMPLETED: _____

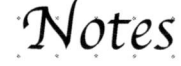
Notes

DATE STARTED: _____

PROJECT:_____

MATERIALS

BASE MATERIAL AND SIZE:_____

COLORS

_____
_____
_____
_____
_____
_____
_____
_____

ADDITIVES

_____
_____
_____

TECHNIQUES USED

_____
_____
_____
_____
_____

CURING TIME/COMPLETED _____

FINISH MATERIALS/TECHNIQUE

_____
_____
_____

COMPLETED: _____

Notes

DATE STARTED: _____

PROJECT:_____

MATERIALS

BASE MATERIAL AND SIZE:_____

COLORS

_____
_____
_____
_____
_____
_____
_____

ADDITIVES

_____
_____
_____

TECHNIQUES USED

_____
_____
_____
_____
_____

CURING TIME/COMPLETED _____

FINISH MATERIALS/TECHNIQUE

_____
_____
_____

COMPLETED: _____

Notes

DATE STARTED: _____

PROJECT:_____

MATERIALS

BASE MATERIAL AND SIZE:_____

COLORS

_____
_____
_____
_____
_____
_____
_____

ADDITIVES

_____
_____
_____

TECHNIQUES USED

_____
_____
_____
_____
_____

CURING TIME/COMPLETED _____

FINISH MATERIALS/TECHNIQUE

_____
_____
_____

COMPLETED: _____

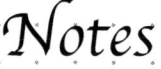
Notes

DATE STARTED: _____

PROJECT:_____

MATERIALS

BASE MATERIAL AND SIZE:_____

COLORS

_____
_____
_____
_____
_____
_____
_____
_____

ADDITIVES

_____
_____
_____

TECHNIQUES USED

_____
_____
_____
_____
_____

CURING TIME/COMPLETED _____

FINISH MATERIALS/TECHNIQUE

_____
_____
_____

COMPLETED: _____

Notes

DATE STARTED: _____

PROJECT:_____

MATERIALS

BASE MATERIAL AND SIZE:_____

COLORS

_____
_____
_____
_____
_____
_____
_____
_____

ADDITIVES

_____
_____
_____

TECHNIQUES USED

_____
_____
_____
_____
_____

CURING TIME/COMPLETED _____

FINISH MATERIALS/TECHNIQUE

_____
_____
_____

COMPLETED: _____

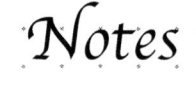

Notes

DATE STARTED: _____

PROJECT:_____

MATERIALS

BASE MATERIAL AND SIZE:_____

COLORS

_____
_____
_____
_____
_____
_____
_____

ADDITIVES

_____
_____
_____

TECHNIQUES USED

_____
_____
_____
_____
_____

CURING TIME/COMPLETED _____

FINISH MATERIALS/TECHNIQUE

_____
_____
_____

COMPLETED: _____

Notes

DATE STARTED: _____

PROJECT:_____

MATERIALS

BASE MATERIAL AND SIZE:_____

COLORS

_____
_____
_____
_____
_____
_____
_____

ADDITIVES

_____
_____
_____

TECHNIQUES USED

_____
_____
_____
_____
_____

CURING TIME/COMPLETED _____

FINISH MATERIALS/TECHNIQUE

_____
_____
_____

COMPLETED: _____

Notes

DATE STARTED: _____

PROJECT:_____

MATERIALS

BASE MATERIAL AND SIZE:_____

COLORS

_____
_____
_____
_____
_____
_____
_____

ADDITIVES

_____
_____
_____

TECHNIQUES USED

_____
_____
_____
_____
_____

CURING TIME/COMPLETED _____

FINISH MATERIALS/TECHNIQUE

_____
_____
_____

COMPLETED: _____

Notes

DATE STARTED: _____

PROJECT:_____

MATERIALS

BASE MATERIAL AND SIZE:_____

COLORS

_____
_____
_____
_____
_____
_____
_____

ADDITIVES

_____
_____
_____

TECHNIQUES USED

_____
_____
_____
_____
_____

CURING TIME/COMPLETED _____

FINISH MATERIALS/TECHNIQUE

_____
_____
_____

COMPLETED: _____

Notes

DATE STARTED: _____

PROJECT:_____

MATERIALS

BASE MATERIAL AND SIZE:_____

COLORS

_____
_____
_____
_____
_____
_____
_____

ADDITIVES

_____
_____
_____

TECHNIQUES USED

_____
_____
_____
_____
_____

CURING TIME/COMPLETED _____

FINISH MATERIALS/TECHNIQUE

_____
_____
_____

COMPLETED: _____

Notes

DATE STARTED: _____

PROJECT:_____

MATERIALS

BASE MATERIAL AND SIZE:_____

COLORS

_____
_____
_____
_____
_____
_____
_____

ADDITIVES

_____
_____
_____

TECHNIQUES USED

_____
_____
_____
_____
_____

CURING TIME/COMPLETED _____

FINISH MATERIALS/TECHNIQUE

_____
_____
_____

COMPLETED: _____

Notes

DATE STARTED: _____

PROJECT:_____

MATERIALS

BASE MATERIAL AND SIZE:_____

COLORS

_____
_____
_____
_____
_____
_____
_____
_____

ADDITIVES

_____
_____
_____

TECHNIQUES USED

_____
_____
_____
_____
_____

CURING TIME/COMPLETED _____

FINISH MATERIALS/TECHNIQUE

_____
_____
_____

COMPLETED: _____

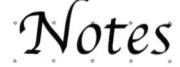

Notes

DATE STARTED: _____

PROJECT:_____

MATERIALS

BASE MATERIAL AND SIZE:_____

COLORS

_____
_____
_____
_____
_____
_____
_____

ADDITIVES

_____
_____
_____

TECHNIQUES USED

_____
_____
_____
_____
_____

CURING TIME/COMPLETED _____

FINISH MATERIALS/TECHNIQUE

_____
_____
_____

COMPLETED: _____

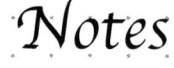

Notes

DATE STARTED: _____

PROJECT: _____

MATERIALS

BASE MATERIAL AND SIZE: _____

COLORS

_____
_____
_____
_____
_____
_____

ADDITIVES

_____
_____
_____

TECHNIQUES USED

_____
_____
_____
_____
_____

CURING TIME/COMPLETED _____

FINISH MATERIALS/TECHNIQUE

_____
_____
_____

COMPLETED: _____

Notes

DATE STARTED: _____

PROJECT:_____

MATERIALS

BASE MATERIAL AND SIZE:_____

COLORS

_____
_____
_____
_____
_____
_____
_____

ADDITIVES

_____
_____
_____

TECHNIQUES USED

_____
_____
_____
_____
_____

CURING TIME/COMPLETED _____

FINISH MATERIALS/TECHNIQUE

_____
_____
_____

COMPLETED: _____

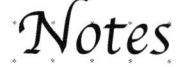

Notes

DATE STARTED: _____

PROJECT:_____

MATERIALS

BASE MATERIAL AND SIZE:_____

COLORS

_____
_____
_____
_____
_____
_____
_____

ADDITIVES

_____
_____
_____

TECHNIQUES USED

_____
_____
_____
_____
_____

CURING TIME/COMPLETED _____

FINISH MATERIALS/TECHNIQUE

_____
_____
_____

COMPLETED: _____

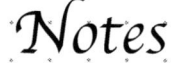

Notes

DATE STARTED: _____

PROJECT:_____

MATERIALS

BASE MATERIAL AND SIZE:_____

COLORS

_____
_____
_____
_____
_____
_____
_____

ADDITIVES

_____
_____
_____

TECHNIQUES USED

_____
_____
_____
_____
_____

CURING TIME/COMPLETED _____

FINISH MATERIALS/TECHNIQUE

_____
_____
_____

COMPLETED: _____

Notes

DATE STARTED: _____

PROJECT:_____

MATERIALS

BASE MATERIAL AND SIZE:_____

COLORS

_____
_____
_____
_____
_____
_____
_____

ADDITIVES

_____
_____
_____

TECHNIQUES USED

_____
_____
_____
_____
_____

CURING TIME/COMPLETED _____

FINISH MATERIALS/TECHNIQUE

_____
_____
_____

COMPLETED: _____

Notes

DATE STARTED: _____

PROJECT:_____

MATERIALS

BASE MATERIAL AND SIZE:_____

COLORS

_____
_____
_____
_____
_____
_____
_____

ADDITIVES

_____
_____
_____

TECHNIQUES USED

_____
_____
_____
_____
_____

CURING TIME/COMPLETED _____

FINISH MATERIALS/TECHNIQUE

_____
_____
_____

COMPLETED: _____

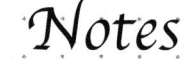
Notes

DATE STARTED: _____

PROJECT:_____

MATERIALS

BASE MATERIAL AND SIZE:_____

COLORS

_____
_____
_____
_____
_____
_____
_____

ADDITIVES

_____
_____
_____

TECHNIQUES USED

_____
_____
_____
_____
_____

CURING TIME/COMPLETED _____

FINISH MATERIALS/TECHNIQUE

_____
_____
_____

COMPLETED: _____

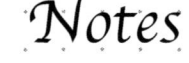

Notes

DATE STARTED: _____

PROJECT:_____

MATERIALS

BASE MATERIAL AND SIZE:_____

COLORS

_____
_____
_____
_____
_____
_____
_____

ADDITIVES

_____
_____
_____

TECHNIQUES USED

_____
_____
_____
_____
_____

CURING TIME/COMPLETED _____

FINISH MATERIALS/TECHNIQUE

_____
_____
_____

COMPLETED: _____

Notes

DATE STARTED: _____

PROJECT:_____

MATERIALS

BASE MATERIAL AND SIZE:_____

COLORS

_____
_____
_____
_____
_____
_____
_____

ADDITIVES

_____
_____
_____

TECHNIQUES USED

_____
_____
_____
_____
_____

CURING TIME/COMPLETED _____

FINISH MATERIALS/TECHNIQUE

_____
_____
_____

COMPLETED: _____

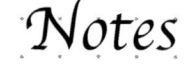

Notes

DATE STARTED: _____

PROJECT:_____

MATERIALS

BASE MATERIAL AND SIZE:_____

COLORS

_____
_____
_____
_____
_____
_____
_____
_____

ADDITIVES

_____
_____
_____

TECHNIQUES USED

_____
_____
_____
_____
_____

CURING TIME/COMPLETED _____

FINISH MATERIALS/TECHNIQUE

_____
_____
_____

COMPLETED: _____

Notes

DATE STARTED: _____

PROJECT:_____

MATERIALS

BASE MATERIAL AND SIZE:_____

COLORS

_____
_____
_____
_____
_____
_____
_____

ADDITIVES

_____
_____
_____

TECHNIQUES USED

_____
_____
_____
_____
_____

CURING TIME/COMPLETED _____

FINISH MATERIALS/TECHNIQUE

_____
_____
_____

COMPLETED: _____

Notes

DATE STARTED: _____

PROJECT:_____

MATERIALS

BASE MATERIAL AND SIZE:_____

COLORS

_____
_____
_____
_____
_____
_____
_____
_____

ADDITIVES

_____
_____
_____

TECHNIQUES USED

_____
_____
_____
_____
_____

CURING TIME/COMPLETED _____

FINISH MATERIALS/TECHNIQUE

_____
_____
_____

COMPLETED: _____

Notes

DATE STARTED: _____

PROJECT:_____

MATERIALS

BASE MATERIAL AND SIZE:_____

COLORS

_____
_____
_____
_____
_____
_____
_____

ADDITIVES

_____
_____
_____

TECHNIQUES USED

_____
_____
_____
_____
_____

CURING TIME/COMPLETED _____

FINISH MATERIALS/TECHNIQUE

_____
_____
_____

COMPLETED: _____

Notes

DATE STARTED: _____

PROJECT:_____

MATERIALS

BASE MATERIAL AND SIZE:_____

COLORS

_____
_____
_____
_____
_____
_____
_____

ADDITIVES

_____
_____
_____

TECHNIQUES USED

_____
_____
_____
_____
_____

CURING TIME/COMPLETED _____

FINISH MATERIALS/TECHNIQUE

_____
_____
_____

COMPLETED: _____

Notes

DATE STARTED: _____

PROJECT:_____

MATERIALS

BASE MATERIAL AND SIZE:_____

COLORS

_____
_____
_____
_____
_____
_____
_____

ADDITIVES

_____
_____
_____

TECHNIQUES USED

_____
_____
_____
_____
_____

CURING TIME/COMPLETED _____

FINISH MATERIALS/TECHNIQUE

_____
_____
_____

COMPLETED: _____

Notes

DATE STARTED: _____

PROJECT:_____

MATERIALS

BASE MATERIAL AND SIZE:_____

COLORS

_____
_____
_____
_____
_____
_____
_____

ADDITIVES

_____
_____
_____

TECHNIQUES USED

_____
_____
_____
_____
_____

CURING TIME/COMPLETED _____

FINISH MATERIALS/TECHNIQUE

_____
_____
_____

COMPLETED: _____

Notes

DATE STARTED: _____

PROJECT:_____

MATERIALS

BASE MATERIAL AND SIZE:_____

COLORS

_____
_____
_____
_____
_____
_____
_____

ADDITIVES

_____
_____
_____

TECHNIQUES USED

_____
_____
_____
_____
_____

CURING TIME/COMPLETED _____

FINISH MATERIALS/TECHNIQUE

_____
_____
_____

COMPLETED: _____

Notes

DATE STARTED: _____

PROJECT:_____

MATERIALS

BASE MATERIAL AND SIZE:_____

COLORS

_____
_____
_____
_____
_____
_____
_____

ADDITIVES

_____
_____
_____

TECHNIQUES USED

_____
_____
_____
_____
_____

CURING TIME/COMPLETED _____

FINISH MATERIALS/TECHNIQUE

_____
_____
_____

COMPLETED: _____

Notes

DATE STARTED: _____

PROJECT:_____

MATERIALS

BASE MATERIAL AND SIZE:_____

COLORS

_____

_____

_____

_____

_____

_____

_____

ADDITIVES

_____

_____

_____

TECHNIQUES USED

_____

_____

_____

_____

_____

CURING TIME/COMPLETED _____

FINISH MATERIALS/TECHNIQUE

_____

_____

_____

COMPLETED: _____

Notes

DATE STARTED: _____

PROJECT:_____

MATERIALS

BASE MATERIAL AND SIZE:_____

COLORS

_____
_____
_____
_____
_____
_____
_____

ADDITIVES

_____
_____
_____

TECHNIQUES USED

_____
_____
_____
_____
_____

CURING TIME/COMPLETED _____

FINISH MATERIALS/TECHNIQUE

_____
_____
_____

COMPLETED: _____

Notes

DATE STARTED: _____

PROJECT:_____

MATERIALS

BASE MATERIAL AND SIZE:_____

COLORS

_____
_____
_____
_____
_____
_____
_____

ADDITIVES

_____
_____
_____

TECHNIQUES USED

_____
_____
_____
_____
_____

CURING TIME/COMPLETED _____

FINISH MATERIALS/TECHNIQUE

_____
_____
_____

COMPLETED: _____

Notes

DATE STARTED: _____

PROJECT:_____

MATERIALS

BASE MATERIAL AND SIZE:_____

COLORS

_____
_____
_____
_____
_____
_____
_____

ADDITIVES

_____
_____
_____

TECHNIQUES USED

_____
_____
_____
_____
_____

CURING TIME/COMPLETED _____

FINISH MATERIALS/TECHNIQUE

_____
_____
_____

COMPLETED: _____

Notes

DATE STARTED: _____

PROJECT:_____

MATERIALS

BASE MATERIAL AND SIZE:_____

COLORS

_____
_____
_____
_____
_____
_____
_____
_____

ADDITIVES

_____
_____
_____

TECHNIQUES USED

_____
_____
_____
_____
_____

CURING TIME/COMPLETED _____

FINISH MATERIALS/TECHNIQUE

_____
_____
_____

COMPLETED: _____

Notes

DATE STARTED: _____

PROJECT:_____

MATERIALS

BASE MATERIAL AND SIZE:_____

COLORS

_____
_____
_____
_____
_____
_____
_____

ADDITIVES

_____
_____
_____

TECHNIQUES USED

_____
_____
_____
_____
_____

CURING TIME/COMPLETED _____

FINISH MATERIALS/TECHNIQUE

_____
_____
_____

COMPLETED: _____

Notes

DATE STARTED: _____

PROJECT:_____

MATERIALS

BASE MATERIAL AND SIZE:_____

COLORS

_____
_____
_____
_____
_____
_____
_____

ADDITIVES

_____
_____
_____

TECHNIQUES USED

_____
_____
_____
_____
_____

CURING TIME/COMPLETED _____

FINISH MATERIALS/TECHNIQUE

_____
_____
_____

COMPLETED: _____

Notes

DATE STARTED: _____

PROJECT:_____

MATERIALS

BASE MATERIAL AND SIZE:_____

COLORS

_____
_____
_____
_____
_____
_____
_____

ADDITIVES

_____
_____
_____

TECHNIQUES USED

_____
_____
_____
_____
_____

CURING TIME/COMPLETED _____

FINISH MATERIALS/TECHNIQUE

_____
_____
_____

COMPLETED: _____

Notes

DATE STARTED: _____

PROJECT:_____

MATERIALS

BASE MATERIAL AND SIZE:_____

COLORS

_____
_____
_____
_____
_____
_____
_____
_____

ADDITIVES

_____
_____
_____

TECHNIQUES USED

_____
_____
_____
_____
_____

CURING TIME/COMPLETED _____

FINISH MATERIALS/TECHNIQUE

_____
_____
_____

COMPLETED: _____

Notes

DATE STARTED: _____

PROJECT:_____

MATERIALS

BASE MATERIAL AND SIZE:_____

COLORS

_____
_____
_____
_____
_____
_____

ADDITIVES

_____
_____
_____

TECHNIQUES USED

_____
_____
_____
_____
_____

CURING TIME/COMPLETED _____

FINISH MATERIALS/TECHNIQUE

_____
_____
_____

COMPLETED: _____

Notes

DATE STARTED: _____

PROJECT:_____

MATERIALS

BASE MATERIAL AND SIZE:_____

COLORS

_____
_____
_____
_____
_____
_____
_____

ADDITIVES

_____
_____
_____

TECHNIQUES USED

_____
_____
_____
_____
_____

CURING TIME/COMPLETED _____

FINISH MATERIALS/TECHNIQUE

_____
_____
_____

COMPLETED: _____

Notes

DATE STARTED: _____

PROJECT:_____

MATERIALS

BASE MATERIAL AND SIZE:_____

COLORS

_____
_____
_____
_____
_____
_____
_____

ADDITIVES

_____
_____
_____

TECHNIQUES USED

_____
_____
_____
_____
_____

CURING TIME/COMPLETED _____

FINISH MATERIALS/TECHNIQUE

_____
_____
_____

COMPLETED: _____

Notes

DATE STARTED: _____

PROJECT:_____

MATERIALS

BASE MATERIAL AND SIZE:_____

COLORS

_____
_____
_____
_____
_____
_____
_____
_____

ADDITIVES

_____
_____
_____

TECHNIQUES USED

_____
_____
_____
_____
_____

CURING TIME/COMPLETED _____

FINISH MATERIALS/TECHNIQUE

_____
_____
_____

COMPLETED: _____

Notes

DATE STARTED: _____

PROJECT:_____

MATERIALS

BASE MATERIAL AND SIZE:_____

COLORS

_____
_____
_____
_____
_____
_____
_____

ADDITIVES

_____
_____
_____

TECHNIQUES USED

_____
_____
_____
_____
_____

CURING TIME/COMPLETED _____

FINISH MATERIALS/TECHNIQUE

_____
_____
_____

COMPLETED: _____

Notes

DATE STARTED: _____

PROJECT:_____

MATERIALS

BASE MATERIAL AND SIZE:_____

COLORS

_____
_____
_____
_____
_____
_____
_____

ADDITIVES

_____
_____
_____

TECHNIQUES USED

_____
_____
_____
_____
_____

CURING TIME/COMPLETED _____

FINISH MATERIALS/TECHNIQUE

_____
_____
_____

COMPLETED: _____

Notes

DATE STARTED: _____

PROJECT:_____

MATERIALS

BASE MATERIAL AND SIZE:_____

COLORS

_____
_____
_____
_____
_____
_____
_____

ADDITIVES

_____
_____
_____

TECHNIQUES USED

_____
_____
_____
_____
_____

CURING TIME/COMPLETED _____

FINISH MATERIALS/TECHNIQUE

_____
_____
_____

COMPLETED: _____

Notes

DATE STARTED: _____

PROJECT:_____

MATERIALS

BASE MATERIAL AND SIZE:_____

COLORS

_____
_____
_____
_____
_____
_____
_____

ADDITIVES

_____
_____
_____

TECHNIQUES USED

_____
_____
_____
_____
_____

CURING TIME/COMPLETED _____

FINISH MATERIALS/TECHNIQUE

_____
_____
_____

COMPLETED: _____

Notes

DATE STARTED: _____

PROJECT:_____

MATERIALS

BASE MATERIAL AND SIZE:_____

COLORS

_____
_____
_____
_____
_____
_____

ADDITIVES

_____
_____
_____

TECHNIQUES USED

_____
_____
_____
_____
_____

CURING TIME/COMPLETED _____

FINISH MATERIALS/TECHNIQUE

_____
_____
_____

COMPLETED: _____

Notes

DATE STARTED: _____

PROJECT:_____

MATERIALS

BASE MATERIAL AND SIZE:_____

COLORS

_____
_____
_____
_____
_____
_____
_____

ADDITIVES

_____
_____
_____

TECHNIQUES USED

_____
_____
_____
_____
_____

CURING TIME/COMPLETED _____

FINISH MATERIALS/TECHNIQUE

_____
_____
_____

COMPLETED: _____

Notes

DATE STARTED: _____

PROJECT:_____

MATERIALS

BASE MATERIAL AND SIZE:_____

COLORS

_____
_____
_____
_____
_____
_____
_____

ADDITIVES

_____
_____
_____

TECHNIQUES USED

_____
_____
_____
_____
_____

CURING TIME/COMPLETED _____

FINISH MATERIALS/TECHNIQUE

_____
_____
_____

COMPLETED: _____

Notes

DATE STARTED: _____

PROJECT:_____

MATERIALS

BASE MATERIAL AND SIZE:_____

COLORS

_____
_____
_____
_____
_____
_____
_____

ADDITIVES

_____
_____
_____

TECHNIQUES USED

_____
_____
_____
_____
_____

CURING TIME/COMPLETED _____

FINISH MATERIALS/TECHNIQUE

_____
_____
_____

COMPLETED: _____

Made in the USA
Middletown, DE
29 November 2019